# the BLACK EYED PEAS

T0027185

**Gareth Stevens**
Publishing

By Molly Shea

**Please visit our Web site, www.garethstevens.com. For a free color catalog of all our high-quality books, call toll free 1-800-542-2595 or fax 1-877-542-2596.**

Library of Congress Cataloging-in-Publication Data

Shea, Molly.
The Black Eyed Peas / Molly Shea.
     p. cm. — (Hip-hop headliners)
Includes index.
ISBN 978-1-4339-4792-6 (library binding)
ISBN 978-1-4339-4793-3 (pbk.)
ISBN 978-1-4339-4794-0 (6-pack)
1.  Black Eyed Peas (Musical group)—Juvenile literature. 2.  Rap musicians—United States—Biography—Juvenile literature. I. Title.
ML3930.B577S54 2011
782.42164092'2—dc22
[B]

                                     2010023236

First Edition

Published in 2011 by
**Gareth Stevens Publishing**
111 East 14th Street, Suite 349
New York, NY 10003

Copyright © 2011 Gareth Stevens Publishing

Designer: Haley W. Harasymiw
Editor: Therese Shea

Photo credits: Cover background, background pp. 2–32 Shutterstock.com; cover (Black Eyed Peas), p. 1 Charles Eshelman/FilmMagic; p. 5 Michelly Rall/Getty Images for Live Earth Events; p. 7 Carl De Souza/Getty Images; p. 9 Scott Gries/Getty Images; p. 11 M. Caulfield/WireImage for NARAS; p. 13 SGranitz/WireImage; p. 15 Des Willie/Redferns; p. 17 KMazur/WireImage; p. 19 Jo Hale/Getty Images; p. 21 Mayela Lopes/AFP/Getty Images; pp. 23, 25 Kevin Winter/Getty Images; p. 27 Simone Joyner/Getty Images; p. 29 Dan MacMedan/WireImage.

CPSIA compliance information: Batch #CW11GS: For further information contact Gareth Stevens, New York, New York at 1-800-542-2595.

# Contents

# Meet the Peas

The Black Eyed Peas make fun hip-hop music. The group's members are will.i.am, apl.de.ap, Taboo, and Fergie.

will.i.am

Taboo

Fergie

apl.de.ap

# Forming the Group

In 1988, eighth-graders Will Adams and Allen Pineda began rapping together. Now their names are will.i.am and apl.de.ap!

The two boys started working on music. They formed a group called Atban Klann. They changed the name to the Black Eyed Peas in 1995.

Jaime Gomez joined the Black Eyed Peas. Today he is known as Taboo. A singer named Kim Hill also sang with them.

# The Albums

The Black Eyed Peas' first album was released in 1998. It was called *Behind the Front*. The second album was called *Bridging the Gap*.

13

Fans loved the Black Eyed Peas' concerts. They were different from other hip-hop groups. They sang and danced. They had a band.

For their third album, Stacy Ferguson sang with the group. "Fergie" gave them a new sound.

The 2003 album *Elephunk* was a huge hit. The group sang "Where Is the Love?" with Justin Timberlake.

The album *Monkey Business* came out in 2005. The song "Don't Phunk with My Heart" was the biggest hit.

# Fergie Solo

In 2006, Fergie released a solo album called *The Dutchess*. It had three number-one hits. Fergie then returned to the Black Eyed Peas.

# The E.N.D.

The Black Eyed Peas called their fifth album *The E.N.D.* This stands for "The Energy Never Dies."

The song "Boom Boom Pow" was the Black Eyed Peas' first number-one hit. It stayed on top for 12 weeks in a row. "I Gotta Feeling" was a number-one hit, too!

The Black Eyed Peas won three Grammys in 2010. They also put out another album called *The Beginning* that year. They make music that keeps people dancing!

# Timeline

**1988**    will.i.am and apl.de.ap start working together.

**1995**    Taboo joins the Black Eyed Peas.

**1998**    The first album, *Behind the Front*, is released.

**2003**    Fergie joins the Black Eyed Peas.

**2006**    Fergie's solo album, *The Dutchess*, comes out.

**2009**    "Boom Boom Pow" becomes the group's first number-one hit.

**2010**    The Black Eyed Peas win three Grammys. *The Beginning* comes out.